In memory of my parents, Rachel and Yehuda Shifman

————

I would like to thank William Broecker, my teacher and mentor, for his gentle guidance during this project; John Crowley, for believing in my work and for bringing it to Abrams; Raymond Hooper, for his wonderful design; Harriet Whelchel, for being both editor and friend; Ethan Silverman, for his artistic contribution and knowledge of the theater; and Harold Prince, for making his thoughts and his love of theater a part of my book;

and especially

Moshe Katvan, my husband, who stood by me and supported me during this project, and Danielle Katvan, my daughter, who encouraged me to go backstage again and to keep making images.

—RSK

Page 2: Susan Taylor, Victoria Lectacave, Kristen Olness, Christina Pawl, *Cabaret*, 1998

Editor: Harriet Whelchel
Designer: Raymond P. Hooper

Library of Congress Cataloging-in-Publication Data

Katvan, Rivka Shifman.
    Backstage : Broadway behind the curtain / photographs by Rivka Shifman Katvan ; foreword
  by Harold Prince ; introduction by Ethan Silverman.
      p.   cm.
    Includes index.
    ISBN 0–8109–5709–4
    1. Theater—New York (State)—New York—Pictorial works. 2. Actors—New York
(State)—New York—Portraits. I. Title.

    PN2277.N5 K36 2000
    792'.09747'1—dc21

                                                                00–063978

Published in 2001 by Harry N. Abrams, Incorporated, New York

Printed and bound in Hong Kong

Harry N. Abrams, Inc.
100 Fifth Avenue
New York, N.Y. 10011
www.abramsbooks.com

Contents

FOREWORD Harold Prince   6

INTRODUCTION Ethan Silverman   14

BACKSTAGE   20

INDEX OF PLAYS   136

Foreword

I've been quoted—accurately—as saying that I prefer black-and-white film to Technicolor and silent films to talkies. Following that trajectory, I suppose I prefer still black-and-white photographs to moving pictures.

Why?

It's a matter of imagination—a compact between subject and viewer. Every still photograph carries with it an infinite subtext. Who or what is the subject? Why is it a subject? What is its past? What could be its future? What about its surroundings? What of the additional senses—smell, sound, taste, touch—that inform the subject of a still photograph?

Such things make living theater. And over a lifetime in the theater, I have incorporated still photographs not only in the development of text, but also, and equally important, during the design process.

Rivka Katvan's photographs honor the same priorities that motivate my work. She takes a picture and invites you to experience it. There is sadness and then exhilaration in almost everything she photographs; an aftertaste. The viewer is her collaborator, just as the audience is mine. Without fuss or self-consciousness, without undue editorializing, she captures in this book working people at their jobs.

At Rivka's request, I'm limiting my comments to those photographs of shows on which (I suppose you could say) we worked together. Each reminds me of a specific moment. And the subject of each photograph undoubtedly would be reminded of something quite different. So still photography animates memory and imagination in profound ways.

Harold Prince

Harold Prince, Tony Awards, 1999

Clockwise from floor: James Bonkovsky, David Shine, Liz Callaway, David Louis, Lonny Price, Harold Prince, James Weissenbach, Tom Shea, Daisy Prince Chaplin, Jason Alexander, Terry Finn

This is a picture taken in the early stages of *Merrily We Roll Along* (1982). If you look carefully, you will find Jason Alexander, who was nineteen at the time and, in Stephen Sondheim's, George Furth's, and my opinion, well on his way to being the Edward G. Robinson of films. Well, we may have been wrong on the specifics, but we were certainly right in terms of his huge success. The young lady, sixteen years old at the time, kneeling to hear my notes, is my daughter, Daisy Prince Chaplin. It was both a wonderful and incredibly painful experience for me, that show, in that I let it down because I never really got a handle on how to direct it.

Craig Lucas and Robert Henderson, *Sweeney Todd,* 1979

Clearly, these high jinks "backstage at *Sweeney Todd"* were posed especially for Rivka's camera. The only reason I include this picture is because the gentleman in the foreground, who played bit parts, sang wonderfully, and with whom I worked on other Broadway shows, a very few years later became the prestigious American playwright Craig Lucas, whose work is performed on stages all over the world.

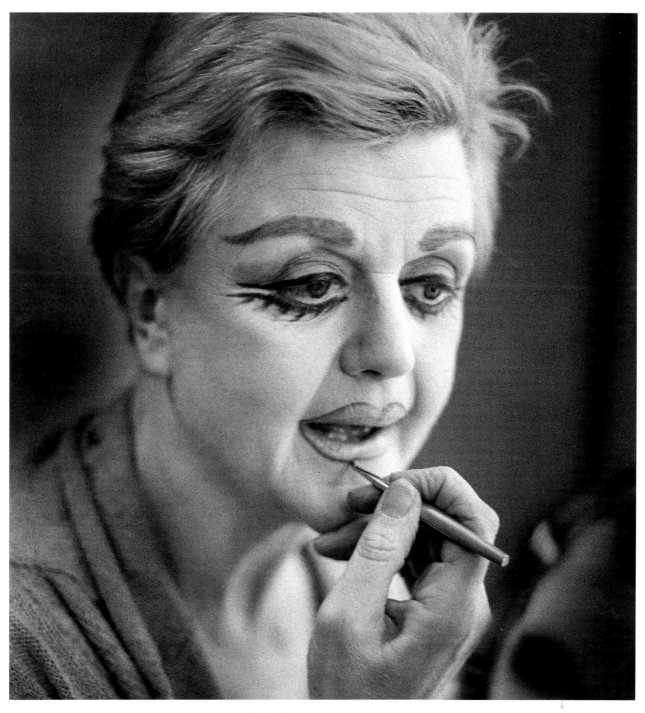

These two pictures represent "before" and "after." Angela Lansbury, the consummate professional, is taking on Nellie Lovett (*Sweeney Todd,* 1979). On completing the makeup, she is the character.

Angela Lansbury . . .

Presto Changeo . . .

Mrs. Lovett

*B*ackstage—the word can conjure up an image of a privileged place where secrets exist and magic happens. Or it can literally define the unadorned series of hallways and rooms with exposed pipes and peeling paint that hold "the works" of a theater. In the land of make-believe, plays and movies, we have seen many versions of backstage life (some more believable than others). In reality, it is a place that is usually off-limits to the audience. And that is the way it should be, for it is backstage that the land of make-believe is created. The intent is for the audience to experience the fantasy from the other side of the footlights.

Think about the most colorful and beautiful musical you have ever seen, and then think about the most utilitarian and least decorated building you have been in. That's the physical contrast I experienced as a young man in the 1970s, when I went backstage for the first time. My most vivid memory, however, was the feeling of excitement in the air, the juices of creativity flowing through the cramped quarters. A few years later, when I was nineteen and in my first professional job, as the assistant director of *The Elephant Man* at the Booth Theatre, my favorite place was backstage. When John Thomas waved me through, and I was allowed to wander freely behind, beside, over, and under a Broadway stage, I knew I was working in the theater. That actually meant more to me than being able to walk into the theater for free.

Most Broadway theaters are old, which may account for the feeling of a cramped tenement backstage. There are few "star" dressing rooms. Those that exist are highly coveted; most are shared. The area that is occupied by

the crew is usually beneath the stage, an even more crowded area. The technical state of production has exceeded the architecture of these buildings, and the two worlds meeting is a millennial challenge of space usage. Interestingly enough, the more modern and technically advanced the building, the less character and charm the theater possesses, in front of and behind the stage.

The feeling of backstage, of course, depends not only on the architecture of the theater itself, but also on the show that is being performed and the people who are working on it. Some shows that are full of life and spirit onstage are in sharp contrast to the dreary and depressing atmosphere backstage, and some dark and imposing plays are marked with giddiness and joy behind the scenes. During some shows, all the dressing-room doors are open, with people and music flowing in and out. During others, the doors are shut and solemnity rules the day. Each backstage is its own world, with its own rules. Dressing rooms become like homes, though of course they aren't. The hallways become places of performance, but with no audience. Backstage must accommodate all these contradictions because it is where the actors must become the characters they are to play. And this is the one thing that all backstage areas have in common: they are places of transformation, where the actors leave the street and their home lives to enter the world of the show.

Actors are often accused of always being "on," of showing very little distinction between performance and reality. On the following pages, Rivka Katvan's photographs will reveal that as a fallacy. By the time an actor is

John Thomas,
backstage doorman
at the Booth Theatre,
c. 1979

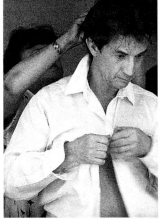

Clockwise from center: Sarah Rice, *Sweeney Todd,* 1979; Martin Short, Tony Awards, 1999; *(left to right)* dresser Robert Miller, Mary Testa holding Lillias White's baby, Navarre Matlovsky, dresser David Dumais, Fred Garbo Garver, Terrence Mann, *Barnum,* 1980; Kevin Spacey and Jason Robards, Tony Awards, 1999; James Valentine, *Camelot,* 1980; Mandy Patinkin, Tony Awards, 2000; Elaine Stritch, Tony Awards, 1999; *(left to right)* Keith Davis, Joseph Wise, Quitman Fludd III, Ray Stephens, *On the Twentieth Century,* 1978; Anna Friel, *Closer,* 1999

ready to perform in the run of a show, he or she will have spent many weeks in rehearsal with the director, shaping the character. For an actual performance, the final elements come into place: costumes, makeup, and possibly wigs are added to complete the equation and to bring the character to life. These photographs follow the course of that transformation, a process by which magic is created. Looking at a photograph is, in itself, a private and intimate act. Looking at Rivka's photographs provides a glimpse into the private world of the theater.

An actor arrives at the theater and, most likely, enters through the back or side of the building through what is known as the stage door. The men who guard this door, from their post just inside, have seen it all, and they greet these performers on their way to work with a complicit nod. As they cross the threshold and sign in, the actors may be preoccupied with a myriad of things: What happened at home that day? How long will this job last? Some actors seem to be carrying their characters with them as they are walking down the street. Most are completely indistinguishable from

Karen Akers, *Nine*, 1982

everyone else in traffic or on the subway during what is a reverse commute at the end of the day. But once inside the theater, they must corral whatever thoughts are racing through their brains into one direction: that of preparation for the performance.

Once a show is up and running, the Actor's Equity rule for arrival is a half hour before performance time. Few actors adhere to such short notice, and some arrive as early as two hours before "curtain up." Preparation surely begins at home but most performers do their most intense physical stretching and vocalizing at the theater. Of course, there are actors who barely make it on time, sending the stage managers into paroxysms of worry. The age of beepers and cell phones have diminished some of this preshow anxiety caused by traffic jams, oversleep, and the everyday chaos of life.

For every performer, the ritual begins differently: undressing, warming up, costume, and makeup. Everyone has his or her own way and order, and usually it doesn't change once a comfortable groove is found.

And all of this happens in front of a mirror. Mirrors play a big role in all our lives, but not quite in the same way that they do for actors. The relationship that actors have with themselves is something that is often made fun of, but in reality this is not simple narcissism. In order for actors to transform themselves for their roles, they must first confront themselves as they appear and then take that self-awareness and mold it into a character. And it is, often, literally in the reflection of the mirror that the process takes place.

Thus, the actors first see themselves as themselves. Unless, the makeup job requires special skill with complicated prostheses, most actors are required to apply their own makeup. As they see their own unmade-up image in the mirror, they use the physical act of painting their faces to help transform the person into the character. It all depends on each actor's process. Look at these photographs carefully. Maybe you can see the change taking place. Look at the actors' eyes, at the way they seem to be studying something "other" in their faces. Maybe it's just concentration to make sure the eyeliner is straight. Maybe. I think something else is happening in that mirror. We can really see it after the makeup is on. I call it "the look," that last-minute checkup, after all the preparatory work is done, the moment before they leave that tiny dressing room, walk down those stairs, into the wings, and onto the stage. The transformation is complete; ahead is the performance. (A few of the photographs here were taken not at plays or musicals but at the Tony Awards, when the performers were actually performing as themselves as presenters. Even then, some inexplicable change takes place in this in-between world of preparation.) This world of transformation extends beyond Broadway and Off Broadway to anti Broadway, with shows like *Hedwig and the Angry Inch* and *The Donkey Show.*

Once the performance begins, this other world continues to unfold backstage, one that comprises concentration, preparation, boredom, and playfulness. The particulars depend on the nature of the run. If a play is in previews and its very future is in question, the company is not so settled, and anticipatory anxiety is in the air. If it is a hit, routines and a sense of home settle in.

When actors inhabit their dressing rooms, they bring parts of their own personalities with them. During the run of *Cabaret,* Alan Cumming's dressing room accumulated bits of his own life with those of his visitor's; a Spice Girl's poster on the ceiling, Madonna's signature in lipstick on the mirror. Outside his dress-

ing room, he ended up creating a beautiful and eccentric garden, one that in some ways mirrored the qualities of the character he was performing onstage.

Actors rarely have only their makeup kits between themselves and their mirrors. Rivka is a great observer of the creative designs—whether they be family pictures or religious icons that blossom around these mirrors and on the tables in front of them. One dressing-room mainstay, the telegram, is virtually outdated, so the photographs that show opening-night Western Unions actually seem quaint and historical now. The little assemblages that frame the mirrors are endlessly fascinating and draw us even further into the private preparations taking place. Natasha Richardson paints her face as Sally Bowles in view of a note from Mike Nichols and an iconographic photograph of Dame Judi Dench preparing to play the part of an actress in David Hare's *Amy's View.* This strikingly simple but deeply layered image takes on its own iconographic status. Observe icon Elizabeth Taylor's concentrated countenance as she goes from Elizabeth Taylor the woman to Elizabeth Taylor the Movie Star, to Broadway Star, to Actress, to Regina in *The Little Foxes,* and back again, all in one simple photograph. And in the photograph of Glenn Close, is she posing for Rivka, getting into character, or camping it up before she goes onstage? Perhaps all of the above.

But in addition to the stars, and they are here in numbers, an entire community of pro-

Elizabeth Taylor, *The Little Foxes,* 1981

Glenn Close, *Barnum,* 1980

fessionals is required to create the magic of a Broadway performance, and they are faithfully represented. The chorus men and women and other supporting players are often crammed into spaces meant for many fewer people, yet they are able to coexist even as they carve out their own spaces. Look at the nuns, showgirls, and circus performers in their various stage of preparation. These are the people who actually take over the general backstage area, stretching on the stairwells, sharing a smoke in the alleyway, playing cards and Scrabble with crew downstairs while waiting to go on.

The stage manager is the captain of the ship, calling cues, from "half hour," to "places," to every light and scenery change that is maneuvered. In this space, and with unbelievable efficiency, cables are pulled, props are placed, and quick costume changes keep the wheels turning. Once a show is running, it is this group that makes it work. The director is relegated to the corps of the audience trying to make sure the magic appears effortless from the other side of the footlights. These pictures make it clear that everyone from wig maker to dresser to stagehand is an important organ in the living anatomy of what's happening on that stage.

After the show, backstage becomes even more crowded, as family and friends come to pay their respects or congratulate or commiserate. Fans are rarely allowed and have to wait outside the stage door. Certain clichés in the theater ring true, and the hierarchy of backstage visits often do live up to them. People often wonder how sincere words of praise are immediately following a show. Often they are. Look at the suite of photographs in Gregory Hines's dressing room, taken after a performance of *Coming Uptown* on pages 130–32.

Rituals prior to leaving the theater vary as much as they do after arrival. The crew members tend to do their jobs and swiftly exit, as do many actors who dress and leave. For many, backstage is were they begin their long wind-down: receiving guests, having drinks, going out to dinner, whatever it takes to work off the energy they have built up in the last few hours. (But go backstage during flu season and you'll see most actors bundling up and running home.) And the next day, when most of the population is at work, actors face a day of rest or additional work, ultimately thinking about where they are headed at dusk. What is the end of the day for the general population is the beginning for them.

A photographer and friend of mine, Malinda Kilmer, called one day to tell me that she had seen some amazing photographs that she wanted to share with me; she was convinced they would be published and that, with my background, I had to get involved. Malinda's enthusiasm was a prelude that I felt would be very hard to live up to. Out of curiosity, and knowing how hard (and against normal procedure) it is for an outsider to gain access to this fairly guarded world, I went to meet Rivka Katvan.

After years of attending the theater, both as an audience member and as a director, nothing prepared me for the beauty and uniqueness of Rivka's pictures. Was it the theme? The subject matter? The composition? Yes, it was those things, and more. It was the combination of those elements with the introduction of something else, something crucial. These photographs are works of art in themselves. After poring through Rivka's extensive collection, I had the opportunity to talk to Rivka about her outlook and methods.

In the late 1970s, Rivka, a student at The School of Visual Arts in New York, was looking for a subject for her final thesis. While visiting her friend Natalie Mosco backstage at *The Magic Show,* she took some pictures in Mosco's dressing room. A casual moment with a friend turned into an obsession. Eventually, Rivka's symbiotic relationships with the actors she photographed led her to more opportunities as many of them moved on to new shows. Gradually her work began to speak for itself. If Rivka could make contact with a performer and show her photographs, that was entree enough, and some of the biggest stars in the world became willing participants in her art.

Working without a flash, Rivka was as quiet as humanly possible. Therefore, once trust was established, her subjects often forgot that she was even in the room. (Considering the size of most dressing rooms, that wasn't easy.) Len Cariou was oblivious to her presence as he created The Demon Barber of Fleet Street (aka Sweeney Todd) in his dressing room. Maureen Stapleton went on with her life, smoking, reading, doing the crossword puzzles, as if she were alone. The photographs that you see here do not lie. These actors are not perform-

ing for the camera: they are simply being. That is part of Rivka's gift.

From Angela Lansbury to stage doormen, all of the people presented here willingly joined Rivka Katvan in a conspiracy of trust over a period of time. The fact that she was able to engender this trust and gain this access is testament to the way she has with those who inhabit the world of the theater. Rivka's own sensitive nature and genuine caring for these people is apparent in her loving but honest portrayals. As you will see, most actors are completely uninhibited with each other, the crew, and, of course, their dressers. Yes, actors appear in various states of undress, and over the years she captured some in unguarded poses. But they agreed to be photographed because they knew they could trust her. Rivka feels that being honest does not mean you have to hurt people. Portraying an intimate moment doesn't mean you just give it away.

These images speak to me as I know they have spoken to most people who have had the good fortune to see them. When I heard there was a plan afoot to publish them, I was not surprised. I certainly felt privileged to be let in on this twenty-two-year secret and to have the wonderfully difficult job, with Rivka, Harriet Whelchel, Ray Hooper, and John Crowley, of editing these photographs. Now Rivka is sharing her secret. I hope you feel as lucky as I do.

Ethan Silverman

Brian Dennehy, Tony Awards, 1999

Ciaran Hinds, *Closer,* 1999

Liam Neeson, *Judas Kiss*, 1998

Easter Bonnet, 1999

Left to right: Navarre Matlovsky, Dirk Lumbard, Terrence Mann, Andy Tierstein, *Barnum,* 1980

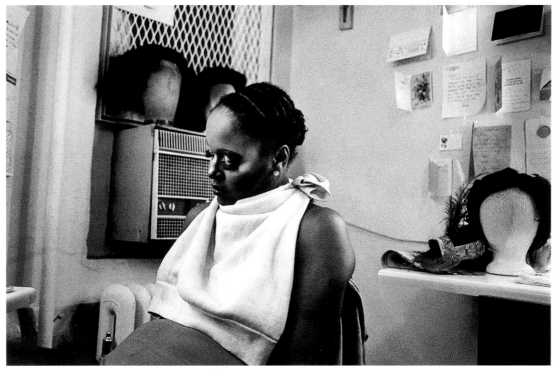

Alaina Reed, *Eubie,* 1978

If actors are dream-makers, these photographs are the shards of our dreams. Because they are in between two realities, they chronicle a rich-yet-occult place: *turiya*, the dream state, those moments between wakefulness, our lives onstage, and "sleepfulness," that place of psychic hibernation where we've removed the makeup and dimmed our creatively focused individuality.

In my photograph, I see makeup, sequins, glued-on lashes, pinned-up hair—all were part of a life I created, of a dream I made come alive. In my dreaming, I was not alone. Other actors were dreaming their dreams with me.

The word "actor" is derived from the Latin *actum*, meaning "a thing done." These photographs are the dreams of our "thing done." They are our family album.

—Natalie Mosco

Natalie Mosco, *The Magic Show,* 1978

Elizabeth Taylor, *The Little Foxes,* 1981

Christine Andreas with dresser Laura Beattie, *The Scarlet Pimpernel,* 1998

Kevin Kline, *On the Twentieth Century*, 1978

Alan Cumming, *Cabaret,* 1998

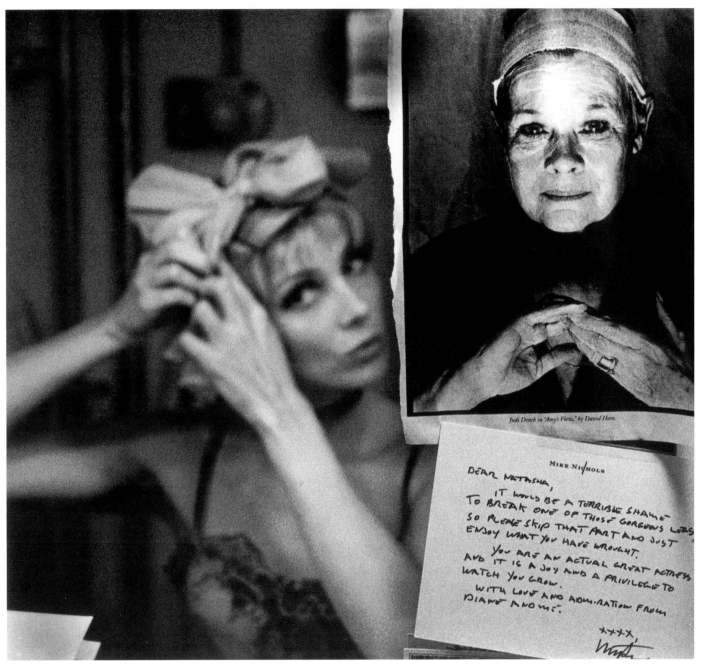

Natasha Richardson, *Cabaret,* 1998

I put this extraordinary "naked" portrait of Judy Dench
up on my mirror to inspire me as I made up before the
performance every night. She's a truly great actress who
was the original Sally Bowles in London.
　　　　　　　　　　　　　　　—Natasha Richardson

Willi Burke, *On the Twentieth Century,* 1978

Coming Uptown, 1979

Jim Dale, *Barnum*, 1980

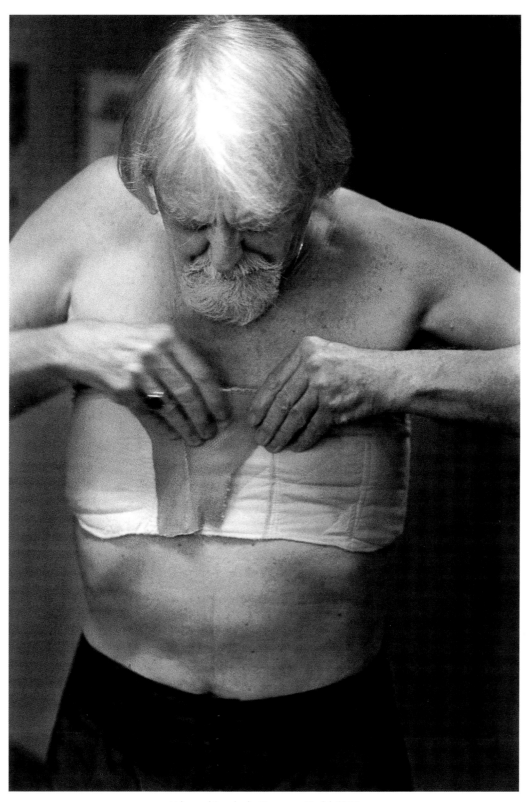

Edmund Lyndeck, *Sweeney Todd*, 1979

Gwen Verdon, *Easter Bonnet*, 1999

Christiane Noll, *Jekyll & Hyde,* 1998

John Barrowman, *Putting It Together,* 1999

Doris Eaton Travis, last living Ziegfeld girl (appeared in 1918 *Ziegfeld Follies*), *Easter Bonnet*, 1999

Dee Hoty, *Easter Bonnet*, 1999

Linda Romoff, Victoria Lectacave, Christina Pawl, Leenya Rideout, *Cabaret*, 1998

Chorus, *Sugar Babies,* 1980

John Benjamin Hickey, *Cabaret,* 1998

Backstage at *Cabaret* was bedlam—a series of
rituals that became more and more obsessive and
intimate as the run continued. If backstage life is
a reflection of, or a reaction to, what is happening
onstage, then you can just imagine what it was like
back there, in the dark. It was a lot of fun.
                    — John Benjamin Hickey

Robert Evan, *Jekyll & Hyde,* 1998

Preparing to play *Jekyll & Hyde* is something
akin to training for a marathon. After each
performance, you feel that you have run an
emotional, vocal, and physical race.

—Robert Evan

The wardrobe rooms and hair rooms backstage are usually where all the action is before, after, and, in some cases, during the show. Sometimes there is more "drama" backstage than onstage. I agree with that great line from the Broadway musical *Applause:* "They should sell tickets to what goes on *backstage*."

—Vincenzo Esoldi

Left to right: Hairstylists Vincenzo Esoldi, Alan Schubert, Ms. Christine, *Barnum,* 1980

Hairstylist Richard Allen, *On the Twentieth Century,* 1978

Michelle Robinson *(left)* and Rosa Curry, *Jelly's Last Jam*, 1993

Stephanie Bast, *The Scarlet Pimpernel,* 1998

Imogene Coca, *On the Twentieth Century*, 1978

This is a surprising photograph of Imogene Coca, one of America's most beloved clowns and a great star with Sid Caesar on television's *Your Show of Shows.* In *On the Twentieth Century*, she plays a dotty old lady ("she's a nut, she's a nut, Mrs. Primrose is a nut"). With enormous, expressive, comic eyes, and a mouth that she twisted to perfection, she perhaps shows in this picture the cost that funny men and women pay for their art.

—Harold Prince

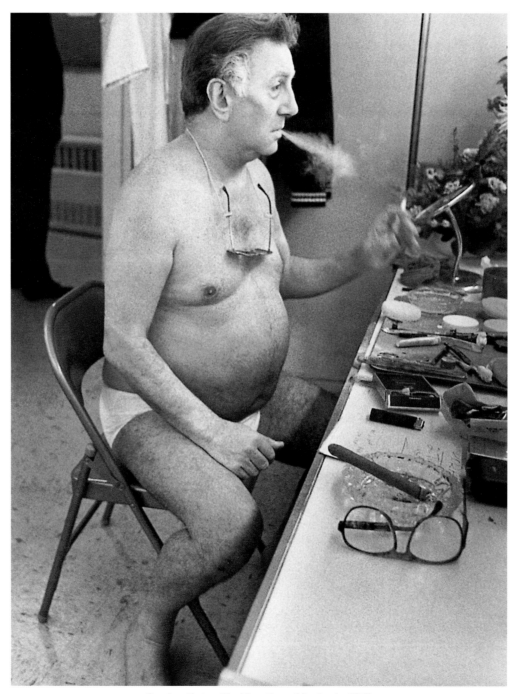

Gordon Chater, *The Elocution of Benjamin,* 1979

Lonnie McNeil, *Eubie,* 1978

Broadway Bares, 1999

Leon Gagliardi, *Broadway Bares*, 1999

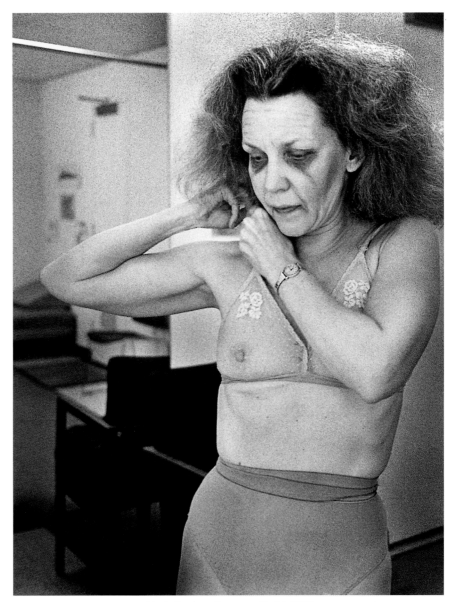

Merle Louise, *Sweeney Todd,* 1979

This is quintessential backstage greasepaint. It is of Merle Louise, the Beggar Lady in *Sweeney Todd*. Seminaked, perhaps, but really naked, as all actors must be to be any good.

—Harold Prince

On the Twentieth Century, 1978

Gwendolyn Coleman, *The Magic Show*, 1978

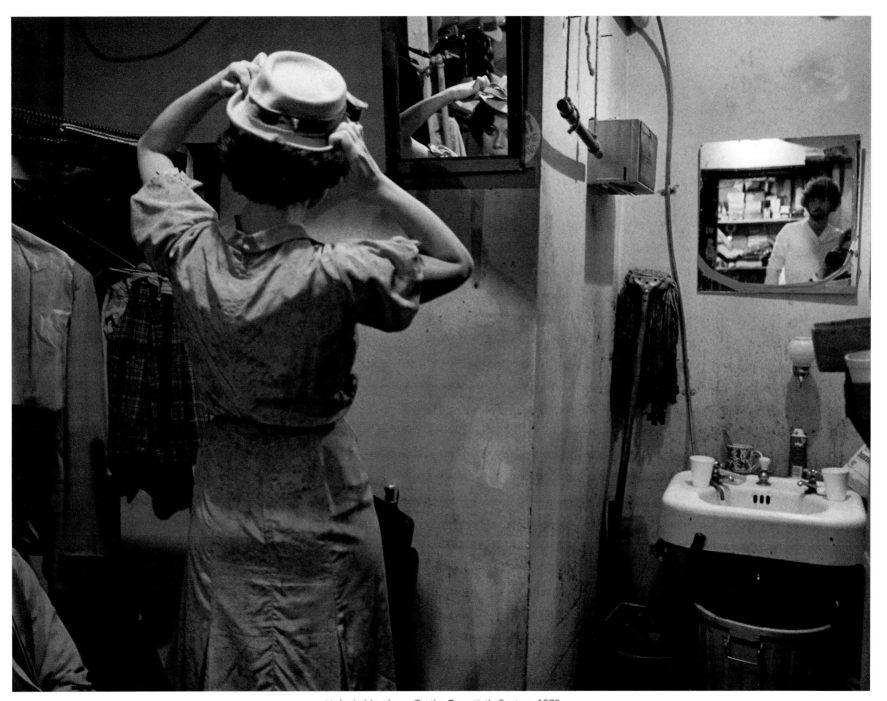

Melanie Vaughan, *On the Twentieth Century,* 1978

Carol Burnett and Julie Andrews, Tony Awards, 1999

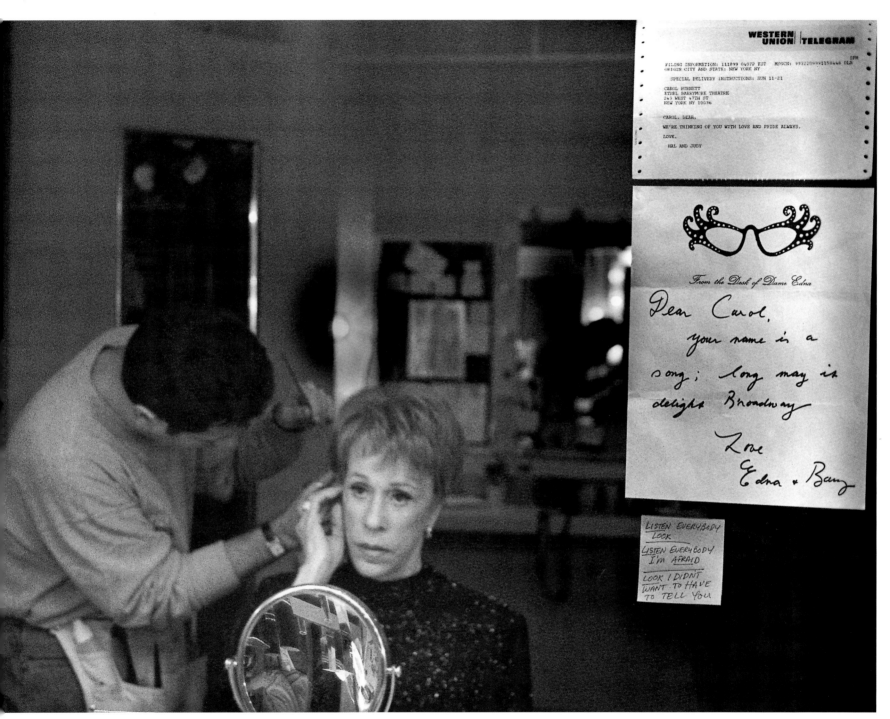

Carol Burnett with hairstylist Alfonso Annotto, *Putting It Together,* 1999

Alan Cumming, *Cabaret*, 1998

Mary Louise Wilson, *Cabaret,* 1998

I love the routines of backstage life: fooling around with the crew;
quick changes, swift, precise, and silent; the nightly, absolutely
necessary rituals of kiss, or joke, or hump before going on.

    The life onstage is fed by the one off. I think the ideal situation
would have all actors in one big dressing room.

—Mary Louise Wilson

Marrianne Tatum and dresser Virginia Lang, *Barnum,* 1980

Douglas Sills, *The Scarlet Pimpernel,* 1998

Betty Buckley, *A Joyous Christmas,* 1999

The afternoon this picture was taken, I'd just come back from visiting Harold Clurman in the hospital (the year was 1981, I believe), and I was feeling very sad. He was such a dear, bright, funny man—a great critic, director, and one of my teachers.
                                    —Elizabeth Wilson

Elizabeth Wilson, *Morning's at Seven,* c. 1981

Douglas Sills, *The Scarlet Pimpernel*, 1998

Terrence Mann and Doug Brown, *The Scarlet Pimpernel,* 1998

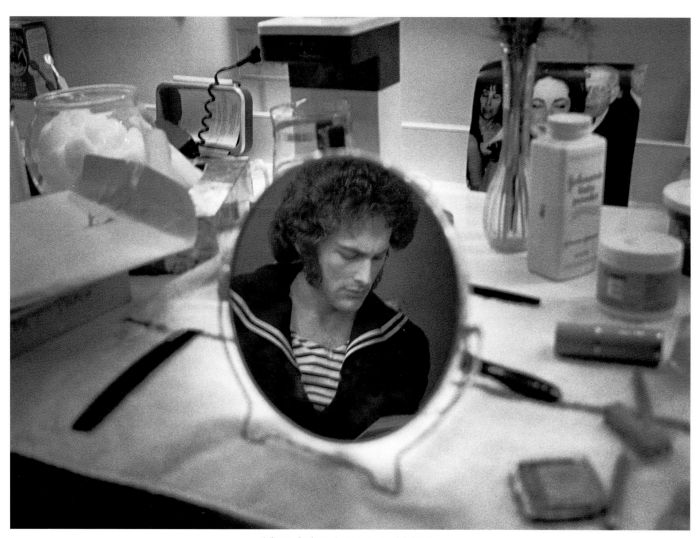

Victor Garber, *Sweeney Todd*, 1979

Left to right: Robbie Morgan, Karen Trott, Sophie Hayden, Catherine Carr, *Barnum*, 1980

Judy Kaye, *On the Twentieth Century*, 1978

Philip Anglim, *The Elephant Man*, 1979

Anna Friel and director Patrick Marber, *Closer*, 1999

Sarah Rice, *Sweeney Todd*, 1979

Anna Friel and Natasha Richardson, *Closer,* 1999

Easter Bonnet, 1999

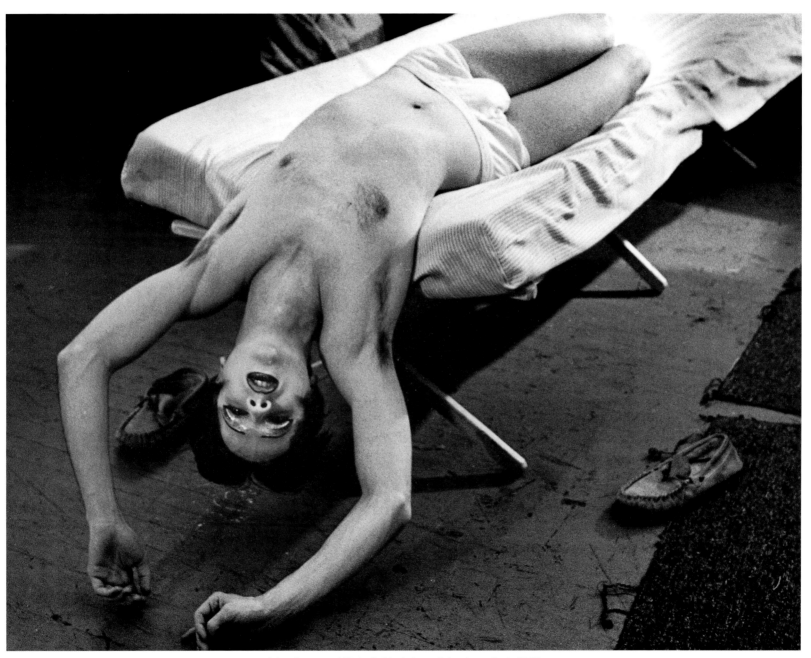

John Cameron Mitchell, *Hedwig and the Angry Inch,* 1998

We sometimes forget that
the pitcher needs time to refill
before you can pour it out again.
Learning how to be still and quiet
onstage as well as off is vital in
maintaining a balance in what
can be a frenetic existence.
　　　　　　　　—Christiane Noll

Christiane Noll, *Jekyll & Hyde*, 1998

Sandy Duncan, *Peter Pan*, 1980

72

Amy Heggins, *Gypsy of the Year*, 1999

Arthur Howard and Gwendolyn Coleman, *The Magic Show*, 1978

Tsidii le Loka, *Nothing Like a Dame*, 1999

Nothing Like a Dame, 1998

Robert Evan, *Jekyll & Hyde*, 1998

Liam Neeson, *Judas Kiss,* 1998

Len Cariou, *Sweeney Todd*, 1979

George Hearn, *Putting It Together*, 1999

Eli Wallach, *Visiting Mr. Green,* 1999

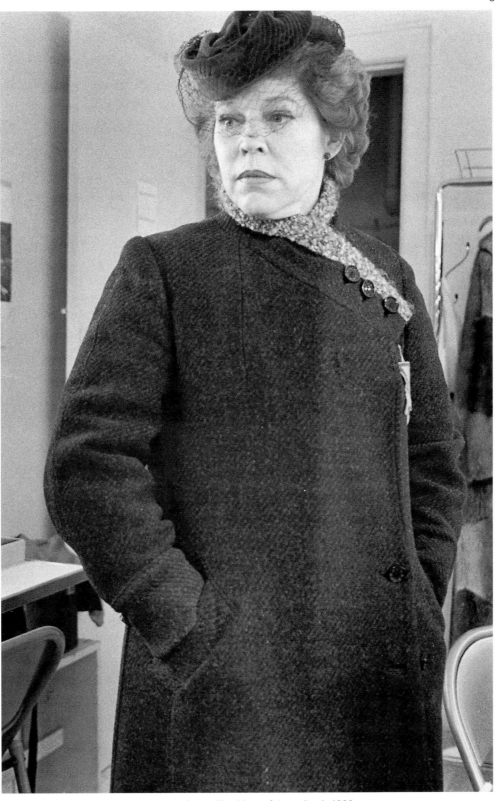

Anne Jackson, *The Diary of Anne Frank*, 1980

Camelot, 1980

Elizabeth Wilson, *Morning's at Seven,* c. 1981

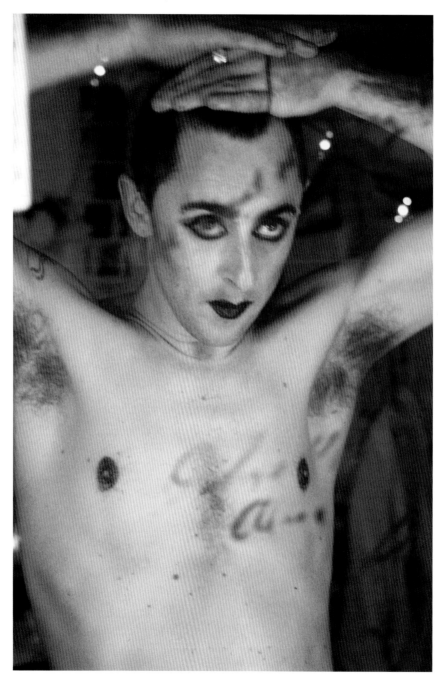

Alan Cumming, *Cabaret,* 1998

Glenn Close, *Barnum*, 1980

In *Barnum*, I played Charity, P.T. Barnum's wife. It was a joyous experience. Led by Jim Dale, our cast was outstanding. Each member of the ensemble was a musician, a juggler, and an acrobat. I learned not only how to walk the tightrope and do the trapeze, but to juggle as well. I also learned something else: No matter how sexy and human I tried to be, it was the vision of my severe grey and black, high-collared dress that the audience took away with them. Sometimes, words cannot transcend the image.

— Glenn Close

Lea Salonga, *Easter Bonnet*, 1999

Heather Headley, *Nothing Like a Dame*, 2000

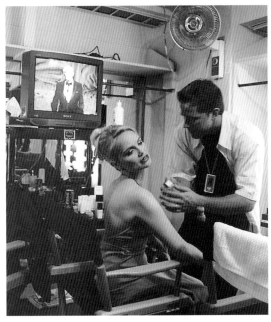

Kristin Chenowith, Tony Awards, 2000

Troy Lambert, *Broadway Bares*, 2000

Keith David, *Jelly's Last Jam*, 1993

Bill Bower and Tom Hewitt, *The Lion King,* 1999

Broadway Bares, 2000

Christine Andreas, *The Scarlet Pimpernel,* 1998

Anna Wilson, *The Donkey Show,* 2000

Nina Goldman (center), *Broadway Bares,* 2000

Our dressing room was an octagonal tower at the top of a hundred-year-old flophouse hotel where the surviving crew of the *Titanic* had taken shelter. I'd take breaks from trowelling on glitter eye shadow with the help of my light-up mirror (set on "twilight") and I'd look over the Hudson River at New Jersey and Ellis Island and the Statue of Liberty and I'd say to myself, "You're home."
—John Cameron Mitchell

John Cameron Mitchell, *Hedwig and the Angry Inch,* 1998

Christine Andreas with dressers Laura Beattie *(left)* and Susan Gustaf, *The Scarlet Pimpernel,* 1998

Anna Friel with dresser, *Closer,* 1999

Tony Awards, 2000

When we arrived at the Kit Kat Klub [where *Cabaret* was performed], I opened a window that hadn't been opened for years and saw a little enclosed roof area, and I just knew that ... it could be transformed into a little garden. And it was. Every day I'd come in early to sit in it and just have some me-time before the show. At the interval, I'd tend to the plants and, immediately afterward, I'd shower in the open air. Then guests and friends would squeeze out through the window and we would have drinks and laugh, lit by candles and Christmas lights. It really was a magical place, and when the show closed down for a month because some scaffolding had collapsed next door, it was really sad for me because I couldn't water my plants, and some of them died.

—Alan Cumming

Alan Cumming, *Cabaret*, 1998

Ruthie Henshall, *Putting It Together,* 1999

One of the many, huge perks of doing a show with Carol Burnett
is her generosity in offering her dressing room as the
company green room. As you can see, I graciously accepted!
—Ruthie Henshall

Natasha Richardson, *Cabaret*, 1998

Carole Shelley, *The Elephant Man*, 1979

Gregory Hines, *Coming Uptown*, 1979

John Cameron Mitchell, *Hedwig and the Angry Inch,* 1998

Mickey Rooney, *Sugar Babies,* 1980

From top: Cabaret's Vance Avery, Michael O'Donnel, Erin Hill, Joyce Chittick, Linda Romoff, Tony Awards, 1998

Leenya Rideout, *Cabaret*, 1998

Kevin Kline and Quitman Fludd III, *On the Twentieth Century,* 1978

So much time backstage is spent sitting around, waiting.
Here, Kevin Kline in his dressing room at *On the Twentieth
Century,* one of the "Pullman porters" in the company, and
Kevin Kline's dresser "shoot the breeze."

—Harold Prince

Ramona Brooks and Arthur Howard, *The Magic Show,* 1978

On the Twentieth Century, 1978

On the Twentieth Century, 1978

Amanda Plummer, *A Taste of Honey,* 1981

Cherry Jones, *A Moon for the Misbegotten,* 2000

Every performance I look up into the fly
and can't believe I'm getting to do what I've
wanted to do all my life, again.

—Cherry Jones

Caitlin Carter, *Nothing Like a Dame,* 2000

Duane Bodin, *Sweeney Todd*, 1979

The Diary of Anne Frank, 1980

Coming Uptown, 1979

Ron Rifkin, *Cabaret*, 1998

Jack Eric Williams, *Sweeney Todd,* 1979

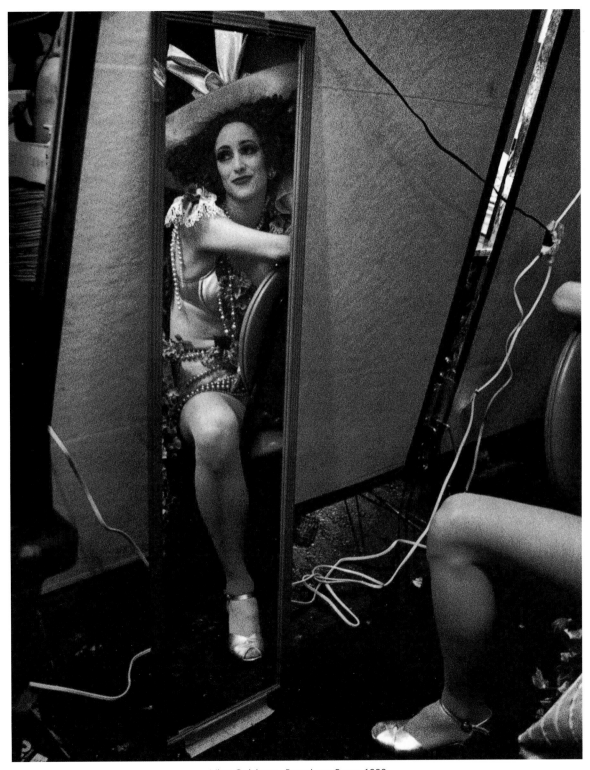

Nina Goldman, *Broadway Bares,* 1999

Left to right: Dirk Lumbard, dressers David Dumais and Dan Lomax, William Witter, *Barnum,* 1980

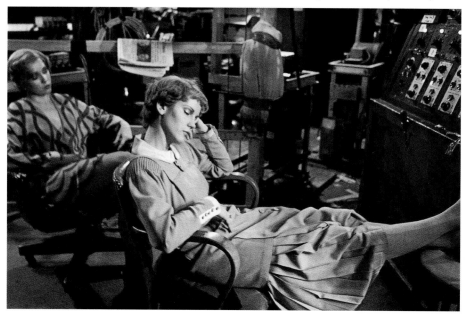

Melanie Vaughan, *On the Twentieth Century,* 1978

Maris Clement and Karen Gibson, *On the Twentieth Century*, 1978

I like this picture, taken backstage, of two ensemble women in *On the Twentieth Century*, because of the obvious contrast of their finery and the necessary grubbiness of backstage accommodations. I'm sure Actor's Equity would object to this comment, but there is something wondrous and dynamic in the contrast between what we show the world and where we put it together. I believe this. Just as I believe that you do your best work on an empty stomach.

—Harold Prince

Richard Hamilton, *Morning's at Seven,* c. 1981

Nancy Marchand, *Morning's at Seven,* c. 1981

Tom Aldredge, *The Little Foxes,* 1981

Carol Lurie and George Coe, *On the Twentieth Century,* 1978

On the Twentieth Century, 1978

Peggy Cooper *(left)* and Sal Mistretta *(stretching), On the Twentieth Century,* 1978

Rita Rudner, *The Magic Show,* 1978

Rufus Smith and Charles Rule, *On the Twentieth Century,* 1978

Melanie Vaughan, *On the Twentieth Century*, 1978

Rupert Graves and Ciaran Hinds, *Closer*, 1999

John W. Bubbles, *Black Broadway*, 1980

Rivka: It's Gregory, I'm calling you back about John Bubbles. He
was confined to a wheelchair during *Black Broadway*—I think he
had a stroke, or a few strokes. He [had a] team called Buck and
Bubbles—he was one of the greatest tap and song-and-dance men
ever. John Bubbles was one of the top three [dancers]: Savion
Glover, Jimmy Slides, John Bubbles, in that order. John Bubbles—
amazing. Dancers were dancing on their toes before John Bubbles
came and put them on their heels.
                                        —Gregory Hines on John Bubbles, June 1999

Eubie Blake and John W. Bubbles, *Black Broadway*, 1980

Christine Ebersole, *Camelot,* 1980

Maureen Stapleton and Joe Ponazecki, *The Little Foxes,* 1981

Julie Harris, *A Joyous Christmas,* 1999

Fred Garbo Garver and Catherine Carr, *Barnum,* 1980

Duane Bodin, *Sweeney Todd*, 1979

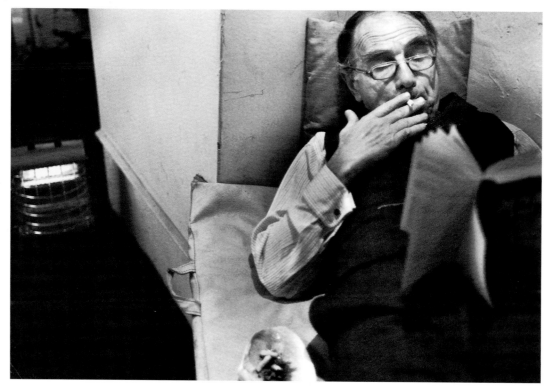

Gary Merrill, *Morning's at Seven*, c. 1981

Novella Nelson, *The Little Foxes*, 1981

Backstage birthday celebration for Maureen Stapleton, being kissed by Anthony Zerbe, *The Little Foxes*, 1981

Gregory Hines and Tom Waits, opening night, *Coming Uptown,* 1979

Gregory Hines and Lena Horne, opening night, *Coming Uptown,* 1979

Gregory Hines and his brother, Maurice, opening night, *Coming Uptown*, 1979

Gregory Hines and Albert Finney, opening night, *Coming Uptown*, 1979

Gregory Hines and his mother, opening night, *Coming Uptown*, 1979

Ron Rifkin's dressing room, *Cabaret*, 1998

It's crazy how quickly the dressing room becomes
my home. A place of safety and comfort—like no
other place in the world.

—Ron Rifkin

Carol Burnett, *Putting It Together*, 1999

It was a night in November, 1954. It was raining hard. I presented myself at the stage door of the theater where *The Pajama Game,* the biggest hit on Broadway, was playing. In the downpour, in my plastic raincoat, I was definitely the poor man's Eve Harrington. The stage doorman, looking like every doorman in those old Betty Grable movies, (whose name was always Pops) pulled me in. I was backstage . . . in an actual Broadway theater!

POPS: Yeah kid, whaddya want?

ME: Well sir, Eddie Foy, Jr., and I have a mutual friend and he told me to look up Mr. Foy. He said Mr. Foy was very nice, and maybe he could give me some advice about how to get into show business.

Eddie Foy, Jr., who cut his teeth on vaudeville, was one of the stars of *The Pajama Game.*

POPS: They're still on stage . . . curtain's down any sec now.

I hear the singing . . . the orchestra . . . and then suddenly, a huge clap of thunder. But it wasn't thunder, it was *applause!* Suddenly, I saw the stars running off into the wings and then back out front, again and again taking their bows. John Raitt, Janis Paige, Carol Hainey, and Eddie Foy, Jr. When they finished, they came off stage and headed for their dressing rooms while the audience was still "Bravo-ing").

POPS (calling to Eddie): Hey Eddie, this kid here wants to see ya!

EDDIE: Yeah kid? Whaddya want?

ME (all in one breath): Mr. Foy-a-friend-of-mine-from-California-where-I-just-came-from-worked-with-you-in-a-movie-he-had-a-bit-part-as-a-cop-remember? Anyhow-he-said-you-were-a-real-swell-guy-and-that-maybe-I-should-ask-you-for-your-advice-on-how-to-get-into-show-business!

EDDIE: You sing?

ME: Kind of. I'm very loud . . .

EDDIE: You dance?

ME: I can jitterbug . . . a little.

EDDIE: Well, maybe I could get you an audition here for a chorus replacement.

ME: But, I can't read music, and I really can't dance.

EDDIE: You can't read music and you can't dance . . . then . . . what?

ME: Well, I'm not good enough for the chorus, so I guess I have to have a "featured" role.

The fact that Mr. Foy didn't laugh me out of the theater proves the point that he was, indeed, a swell guy.

Sometimes being naive can be a blessing because you don't consider the odds . . . you just barrel ahead, totally believing in yourself and the fates.

That night backstage, listening to the audience laughter and applause, gave me more courage than I ever imagined I could conjure up. As a result, "things" happened, and I realized my dream of having "featured" roles.

Whenever I do live theater, I am ever so grateful to hear that laughter and that "thunderclap," because it takes me back to that blessed rainy night. There can be no aphrodisiac in the world as wonderful. "The Smell" and "the Roar" are everything they're cracked up to be.

I still get awfully nervous during those seconds before the curtain goes up . . . but then I'd get nervous if I *didn't* get nervous . . .

God bless the theater. And please let there be a way for it to thrive . . . forever.

—Carol Burnett

I would like to thank all of the people associated with Broadway Cares for making me part of their family.

—Rivka Shifman Katvan

Broadway Cares/Equity Fights AIDS draws upon the talents, resources, and generosity of the American theater community to provide critically needed services for people with AIDS- or HIV-related illnesses across the country. Crucial to our programs are the contributions of actors and backstage crew members who participate in annual benefit performances both on and Off Broadway.

For the last four years, Rivka has wandered, unescorted and unnoticed, through the best of BC/EFA's Broadway fundraising events. In doing so, she has captured for all time the energy, spirit, and mystery of backstage, which come together in a moment to create the magic you see onstage. If, as the audience, you have ever wondered what it's *really* like behind the curtain, you have an unflinching and expert eye in Rivka Katvan.

—Tom Viola, Executive Director, Broadway Cares/Equity Fights AIDS

INDEX OF PLAYS

The photographer, author, and publisher are grateful to all to those who so kindly consented to be photographed. Every effort was made to identify those represented as fully as possible, and we regret any errors or omissions that may have been made. Numbers refer to page numbers.

Barnum: 15, 18, 23, 32, 42, 56, 63, 85, 116, 126
Black Broadway: 122, 123
Broadway Cares/Equity Fights AIDS special events:
    Broadway Bares: 48, 87, 89, 90, 115
    The 13th Annual Easter Bonnet
    Competition: 22, 34, 36–37, 68, 86
    The 10th Annual Gypsy of the Year
    Competition: 72
    A Joyous Christmas: 58, 125
    Nothing Like a Dame: 74–75, 86, 111

Cabaret (1998): 2, 28–29, 38, 40, 54–55, 84, 92–93, 95, 101, 102-3, 107, 113, 133
Camelot (1980): 15, 82, 124
Closer: 15, 20, 66, 67, 91, 121
Coming Uptown: 31, 97, 113, 130–32
The Diary of Anne Frank (1980): 80, 112
The Donkey Show (Off Broadway): 89
The Elephant Man: 14, 64–65, 96
The Elocution of Benjamin: 46
Eubie: 23, 47
Hedwig and the Angry Inch (Off Broadway): 69, 90, 98
Jekyll & Hyde: 35, 41, 70, 76
Jelly's Last Jam: 43, 87,
Judas Kiss: 21, 77
The Lion King: 88
The Little Foxes (1981): 17, 25, 119, 125, 128, 129

The Magic Show: 24, 50, 73, 105, 108, 120
Merrily We Roll Along: 8–9
A Moon for the Misbegotten (2000): 110
Morning's at Seven: 59, 83, 118, 128
Nine: 16
On the Twentieth Century: 15, 27, 30, 42, 45, 50, 51, 64, 104, 106, 116, 117, 119, 120, 121
Peter Pan: 71
Putting It Together: 35, 53, 79, 94, 134
The Scarlet Pimpernel: 26, 44, 57, 60–61, 89, 91
Sugar Babies: 39, 99
Sweeney Todd: 10–13, 15, 33, 49, 62, 66, 78, 101, 112, 114, 127
A Taste of Honey (1981): 109
The 52d, 53d, and 54th Annual Antoinette Perry "Tony" Awards: 7, 15, 19, 52, 87, 92, 100
Visiting Mr. Green: 81